I0424598

This Journal Belongs To:

___